DATE DUE

	JAN 2 4 2006		

HIGHSMITH #45102

NATIVE AMERICAN LEGENDS
SITTING BULL

Don McLeese

Rourke
Publishing LLC
Vero Beach, Florida 32964

www.rourkepublishing.com

PHOTO CREDITS:
©PhotoDisc, Inc. pgs 9, 19, 25
©Library of Congress all other photos

Title page: *A photo of Sitting Bull's family in front of their tipi, taken around 1891*

Editor: Frank Sloan

Cover and page design by Nicola Stratford

Library of Congress Cataloging-in-Publication Data

McLeese, Don.
  Sitting Bull / Don McLeese.
      p. cm. -- (Native American legends)
Summary: A brief biography of the famous leader of the Lakota Sioux who led his people to victory against the United States Cavalry at the Battle of Little Big Horn.
Includes bibliographical references and index.
  ISBN 1-58952-730-5 (hardcover)
 1. Sitting Bull, 1834?-1890--Juvenile literature. 2. Dakota Indians--Kings and rulers--Biography--Juvenile literature. 3. Hunkpapa Indians--Biography--Juvenile literature. [1. Sitting Bull, 1834?-1890. 2. Dakota Indians--Biography. 3. Dakota Indians--History. 4. Hunkpapa Indians--Biography. 5. Indians of North America--Great Plains--Biography. 6. Kings, queens, rulers, etc.] I. Title. II. Series.
  E99.D1S61243 2003
  978.004'9752--dc21

                    2003004356

Printed in the USA

w

Table of Contents

A Famous Chief

No **Native American chief** was more famous than Sitting Bull. He was a leader of the **tribe** known as the **Lakota Sioux**. He was also a holy man to his people. They called him a **medicine man**. They thought he could heal the sick because of special powers given him by God, the **Great Spirit**. They thought he could tell what would happen in the future.

A photograph of Sitting Bull taken around 1885. ➤
The chief is shown with his peace pipe.

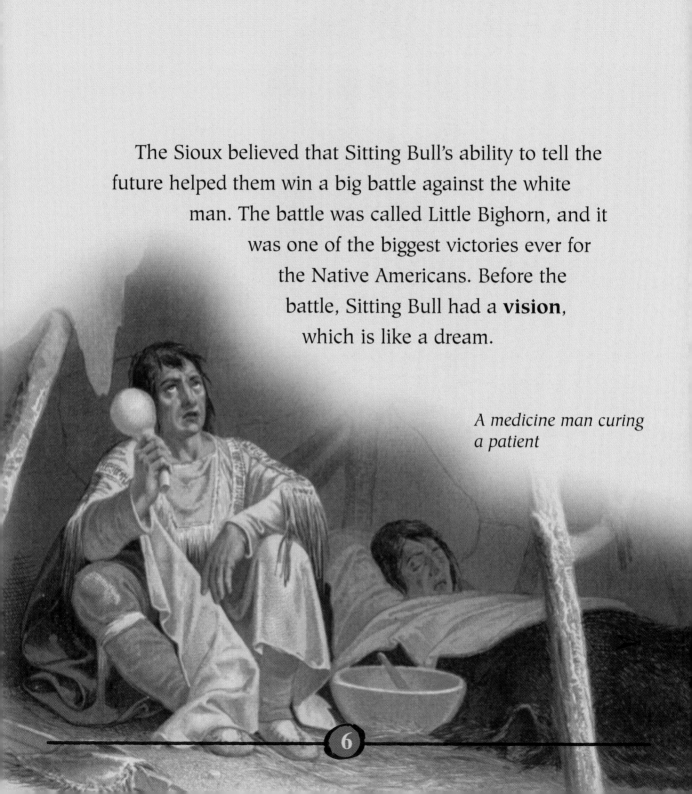

The Sioux believed that Sitting Bull's ability to tell the future helped them win a big battle against the white man. The battle was called Little Bighorn, and it was one of the biggest victories ever for the Native Americans. Before the battle, Sitting Bull had a **vision**, which is like a dream.

A medicine man curing a patient

He thought the Great Spirit was sending him a message that the Sioux would win. After the Sioux won the Battle of Little Bighorn, both Native Americans and the white men believed that Sitting Bull had special powers.

Medicine Man
A medicine man to Native Americans was more like a minister or priest than a doctor. They believed that healing powers came from the Great Spirit, not from a pill or a drugstore.

Son of a Warrior

Sitting Bull was born in 1831. His tribe lived along the Grand River in what is now South Dakota. His father was a great fighter and hunter known as "Returns Again." He was often away fighting battles or hunting for food, but he always came back.

Sitting Bull spent more time with his mother, who was known as "Mixed Day." Among the Sioux, children were raised mostly by their mothers and other female members of the tribe.

"Many Caches"
The place where Sitting Bull was born was called "Many Caches." A **cache** is like a hiding place, and there were a number of holes in the ground where the Sioux could keep food.

Bison, or buffalo, were common in South Dakota ➤
in the 19th century,

In the Sioux tribe, children were given a name that had something to do with how they acted. When Sitting Bull was born, his parents called him "Slow." As a child, he always took a lot of time thinking before he would talk or do anything. His parents had no idea that the boy they called Slow would grow up to be a great chief.

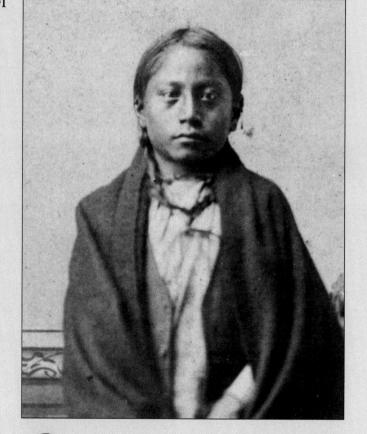

A photo of Crow Foot, ➤
Sitting Bull's own son

Boys in the Sioux tribe played at being hunters and warriors, just like their fathers. They were taught that the Great Spirit had made plants and animals for them to eat and land for them to share. While his father was away, the boy called Slow learned the ways of the Sioux and of the Great Spirit.

The Great Spirit
This was what the Native Americans called their God. They felt that the Great Spirit gave them everything they needed to live. Because the land belonged to the Great Spirit, the Native Americans didn't own it. They shared it.

A New Name

Like most boys, Slow couldn't wait to grow up and become a great **warrior** and hunter like his father. In 1845, when Slow was 14 years old, he watched his father and a number of men leave for a battle. He decided to hop on his pony and follow them! His father was surprised to see his son, but he thought Slow had been very brave to come.

Crow warriors remained on guard against danger. ➤

In the battle with the Crow tribe,
Slow showed he was not afraid.
When the enemy came at him, he
didn't run away. He was like a
strong animal. After the
fighting was over,
his father gave
him a new
name:
Sitting Bull.

Following the Buffalo

The Sioux got most of their meat by hunting the **buffalo**. Buffalo were bigger and stronger than cows. They roamed in packs of hundreds over the area that is now South Dakota, Wyoming, and Montana. The Sioux would follow the buffalo and hunt what they needed for food. They would often have battles with other tribes of Native Americans to see who would get to hunt buffalo and live on the best places to find them.

Native Americans mainly killed buffalo for food and used ➤ their skins for clothing and shelter.

Then white settlers started moving west to the lands where the Native Americans had always lived. The white man wanted to own the land and build houses on it. They also hunted buffalo and drove them away. White settlers who came killed almost all the buffalo, making it harder for the Native Americans to live. The Sioux not only had to fight other Native American tribes, but they also now fought the white man.

As he grew into a man, Sitting Bull was one of the best hunters and warriors in his tribe. In 1856, he became chief of the Strong Hearts, who were the best warriors in the Sioux tribe. They were like the tribe's police and army, keeping the Sioux safe. During a battle with the Crow tribe, Sitting Bull killed the enemy chief, and the Crow tribe ran away.

Sitting Bull was wounded in the leg during the fight, and he would walk with a limp for the rest of his life. But the Strong Hearts knew he had become a great leader. They made him their chief, even though he was only 25 years old.

Crow Tribe
This tribe often fought with the Sioux because they were both hunting buffalo. Both tribes followed the buffalo over what is now South Dakota, Wyoming, and Montana.

◄ *A portrait of Sitting Bull*

Gold

In 1874, a lot more white settlers came to the land where the Sioux lived. They came because they learned that there was a lot of gold in the Black Hills of what is now South Dakota. Gold is a metal that is worth a lot of money. To the Sioux, the Black Hills were a holy land for the Great Spirit. To the white settlers, it was a place where they could become rich.

Sitting Bull had always tried to stay away from the towns where the white people lived and the railroads that took them there. But gold brought so many of them to the Black Hills that it was hard to stay away or scare them away. Both the white settlers and the Native Americans knew that there would be big battles for the land.

The Black Hills of South Dakota, in a recent photograph ➤

Gold Rush

Because gold is very valuable, wherever it was discovered a lot of people came to find more. This was called a "gold rush."

The Sioux village where Sitting Bull lived became one of the largest for Native Americans. There were at least 5,000 warriors there, enough to fight the United States **Cavalry** that wanted to take the land away. One night, Sitting Bull had a vision. As if in a dream, he saw a large army coming to fight the Native American village. But in this vision, all the soldiers in the army were falling into the Sioux village from the sky. It was like they were grasshoppers.

Sitting Bull thought the message of the vision was that these soldiers would die. The Sioux would win the battle. Sitting Bull told the tribe that a battle was coming, but that they shouldn't be afraid. The Great Spirit was on their side.

◄ *A photograph of Sitting Bull taken around 1880*

Another Sioux chief named Crazy Horse believed in Sitting Bull's vision. On June 25, 1876, soldiers led by General George Armstrong Custer attacked the Sioux village near the Little Bighorn River. Crazy Horse was ready for them. He had a lot more warriors than Custer had soldiers. The American soldiers lost and their general was killed. Sitting Bull had been right!

Custer's Last Stand
Another name for the battle is "Custer's Last Stand" because General Custer died during the fight.

General George A. Custer around the time of the battle ➤

The Fight Continues

After Custer lost, thousands more soldiers came to fight the Sioux. Sitting Bull knew that the Sioux couldn't beat the United States Army. In 1877, he led his people into Canada, where the army wasn't allowed to follow. They were safer there, but the weather was very cold. And there were no buffalo to hunt for food. In 1881, Sitting Bull and his tribe returned from Canada and said they wanted peace.

The Little Bighorn Battlefield National Monument ➤

P. FRENZENY

Sitting Bull's Last Days

Because he was so famous, in 1885 Sitting Bull was asked to join Buffalo Bill's Wild West, a traveling show. As part of the show, he would ride around the arena and sign his picture for people who paid him.

Sitting Bull had another vision, which told him he would be killed by his own people. In 1890, there was a gun battle with Native American policemen, and Sitting Bull died. The other Sioux were sad. They knew they had lost a great leader.

Buffalo Bill's Wild West
This was a traveling show about the cowboy way of life run by William "Buffalo Bill" Cody. As part of the play there was a battle with Native Americans who were in the show.

◄ *A painting of William "Buffalo Bill" Cody*

Sitting Bull's People

Sitting Bull was a famous Lakota Sioux chief. The Lakota were a western tribe and were usually called just "Sioux." The Sioux once lived in what is now the southern part of the state of Minnesota. The word "Sioux" is from the French via the Ojibway Indians and means "adder" or "snake."

Today about 60,000 Lakota live on reservations in South Dakota. A few live in the Canadian province of Saskatchewan.

Time Line

1831	✳	Sitting Bull is born.
1845	✳	The boy's first battle changes his name from "Slow" to "Sitting Bull."
1856	✳	Sitting Bull becomes chief of the Strong Hearts.
1874	✳	A "gold rush" brings white settlers west to where the Sioux live.
1876	✳	The Sioux tribe defeats General Custer at the Battle of Little Bighorn.
1877	✳	Sitting Bull leads people to Canada.
1885	✳	Sitting Bull joins Buffalo Bill's Wild West.
1890	✳	Sitting Bull dies.

Glossary

buffalo (BUFF uh loh) — a cow-like animal with short horns and shaggy hair on its neck and back

cache (KASH) — a hiding place

cavalry (KAVV ul ree) — an army group of soldiers riding horses

chief (CHEEF) — leader, head of a Native American tribe

Great Spirit (GRAYT SPEER ut) — the god of many Native American religions

Lakota Sioux (lah KOH tuh SUU) — a tribe of Native Americans, sometimes just called "Sioux"

medicine man (MED uh sin MAN) — a holy man with healing powers

Native Americans (NAY tiv uh MARE ih cans) — those who lived in the land that is now the United States before explorers from Europe came

tribe (TRYB) — one of the bands or nations of Native Americans

vision (VIH zhuhn) — something seen in a dream or a trance

warrior (WAHR ee ur) — a great fighter in battle

Further Reading

Gosda, Randy T. *Sitting Bull*. ABDO Publishing Co., 2002

Roop, Peter and Connie. *Sitting Bull*. Scholastic, Inc., 2002

Todd, Anne M. *Sitting Bull: 1831-1890*. Capstone Press, 2002

Websites to Visit

www.pbs.org/weta/thewest/people/s_z/sittingbull.htm

www.incwell.com/Biographies/SittingBull.html

Index

About The Author

Don McLeese is an award-winning journalist whose work has appeared in many newspapers and magazines. He earned his M.A. degree in English from the University of Chicago, taught feature writing at the University of Texas and has frequently contributed to the World Book Encyclopedia. He lives with his wife and two daughters in West Des Moines, Iowa.